DIVING

GW00854517

Contents

FOREWORD

Diving is fun—this is the theme of this book which comes at a time when interest in diving, and the desire to learn to dive is more popular than at any time in the past.

Learning to dive is a challenge which once accomplished adds a new dimension to the enjoyment of swimming and offers an even more exciting and progressive challenge to those who wish to progress beyond the simple dives.

The co-authors of this book are well aware of the problems and difficulties that can discourage aspiring young divers, particularly when a skilled and knowledgeable coach is not readily to hand. John Wardley and Steve Still have both been coaches to British Olympic Diving Teams. More important each continues to concern himself with the enthusiastic beginner no less than the top performer.

It is because of this that this book has been written with such clarity and understanding and as a result will be of particular help to young divers. The authors are to be congratulated on producing a book which can be read, understood and enjoyed by pupil and teacher alike.

There is no short cut to the mastery of the wide range of dives that are necessary for championship diving. Each new dive successfully attempted is a stepping stone to one more difficult and progress must be continuous if success is to be achieved. The saying 'Nothing ventured, nothing gained', is particularly applicable to diving, and short of being foolish and taking undue risks one should always be prepared to 'have a go' at a new dive.

Peter Heatley, C.B.E., B.Sc., F.I.C.E.,
Hon. Secretary, International Diving Committee

Why Dive?

To most young people, especially children, diving is fun. It adds to the enjoyment of swimming and getting into the water head first is something usually taught in the early stages of learning to swim. The exciting shallow plunge then develops into a long flat dive used to start an energetic swim. As confidence in ones swimming ability grows, so does the desire to dive from higher stages or from spring boards. Many people get a great deal of pleasure from this accomplishment and it is at this stage that Competitive Divers are born. Competitive diving is a form of aerial acrobatics with the additional necessity of controlled entry into water. It is a spectacular sport for participants and viewers, and, because of the ever increasing number of new pools with good diving facilities, it is a fast growing sport. Grace of movement and poise are the requisites of good divers, but these can be developed with training. Confidence in ones capabilities, intelligence, a quick acting brain, and courage are also important factors. Diving is good exercise and a challenging sport. If you wish to learn more about it this book will steer you in the right direction.

Safety

A safe depth of water depends upon the build of the diver; a safe depth for a young child could be dangerous for a fully grown adult. A safe depth of water should allow for a vertical entry of a fully stretched body with arms extended over the head. As the speed of an entry increases with the height of the diving board, greater depth of water is needed for safe entries. In six feet of water, only simple dives by children should be attempted from the pool side, whilst a one metre board should have a depth of ten feet below it. On page 10 you will find details of all recommended board and water depth conditions.

Help

As it is difficult for you to know what is actually happening when you are in mid-air, get a friend to assist you from the pool side. If you are really serious, join a diving club, or contact a diving coach. You may be a future champion!

Confidence Exercises

Some of these shallow water activities are practised when first learning to swim. The main object is to overcome the fear which most beginners feel when attempting to put their heads below water. They will also become familiar with the feeling of being upside down.

1. **Head Ducking.** Stand in shallow water and grasp the hand rail. Bend forward and put your face under the water, holding your breath. Then progress to opening your eyes under the water, and to blowing out your breath before lifting your head out of the water.

2. **Picking up Objects.** Start in shallow water, duck underneath, with the eyes open and pick up coins or other objects from the bottom of the pool. Gradually learn to do this in deeper water so that you have confidence even though you are well below the water surface.

3. **Jumping in.** Jump into the water, remembering to bend the knees to avoid jarring the body when entering shallow water. Try different ways as high as possible, or as far out as possible, but make sure that you are not being a nuisance to someone else.

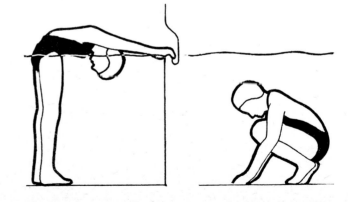

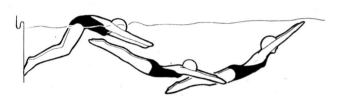

Glide on the Surface

Stand in the shallow water with your back to the wall. Bend forward, bring the legs up behind you, put your head in the water, push hard away from the wall and glide along the surface, with body extended and arms pushed out ahead of you. Stretch your legs and point your toes.

Glide to the Bottom

Repeat the gliding take-off, but point your arms and head towards the bottom of the pool at a shallow angle. From the bottom, push up by using your legs on the pool bottom.

Glide to Armstand

Push and glide along the surface. Then drop the arms and head in a steep angle and reach for the bottom. As the hands touch, lift the legs, stretch them upwards and together to perform an armstand.

Starting to Dive Head-first

With the confidence gained from the shallow water exercises, you can now start diving from the bath side into water between three and five feet deep.

Sitting Dive

Sit on the edge of the pool with the feet resting on the rail or scum channel. Extend the arms towards the water, lower your head, keep your arms pressed together, and your legs closed. Overbalance into the pool and stretch for the bottom. Try to leave your feet on the rail as long as possible and push your hips upwards. When the top half of your body is going downwards, stretch the legs upwards. Hold your head in line with arms until the bottom is reached in a stretched glide.

Kneeling Dive

Kneel on the bath side on one knee only. The foot of the other leg should have the toes gripping the edge of the pool. Bend the body forwards towards the water until the shoulder touches the knee and extend the arms with the head down, and between them. Overbalance and reach for the bottom. Stretch the legs as the body enters the water. Glide to the bottom.

Lunge Dive

This a progression from the kneeling dive. Put one foot on edge of pool. Grip with the toes. Place the other foot about two feet behind. Bend towards water with the arms and head in line. Overbalance, but lift the rear leg which acts as a counterweight, controlling the rate of topple and the angle of entry. As the hands touch the water, the forward leg is lifted and stretched into line with the other leg.

Pike Fall

This helps you to 'feel' a clean entry. Stand on the bathside with the body bent sharply at the waist and with the legs straight. Extend the arms towards the water, shoulder width apart. Look at a point in the water where the entry is visualised. Topple forwards. Keep your legs straight and point the toes. Bring the hands together as they enter the water. Straighten your body so that it passes cleanly through a 'hole' in water.

Spring Header

The first real dive. Stand on the pool edge. Keep upright and place the arms in a 'Y' position. Bend the knees a little and adopt a slight 'crouching forward' attitude. Start toppling forward, but at the same moment extend the legs in a spring, driving the hips upwards. As you approach the water, bring arms and hands together, and press your legs, now straight, into line with rest of body. Try to get a clean entry with a fully extended body.

The Plain Header

This dive embodies the correct elements of diving. It is often used in school and club competitions, both from the bathside, and from higher boards.

Once again the 'Y' position is adopted, and the toes of both feet grip the bath side. The palms of the hands face forwards, and the fingers are pressed together. An upright body position with your stomach pulled in and chest lifted helps towards a graceful start, although strain must be avoided.

Take-off. Bend the knees but keep your body weight over the balls of the feet, retaining balance. Give a vigorous spring, concentrating on getting the hips upwards. Keep the arms straight and in the 'Y' position.

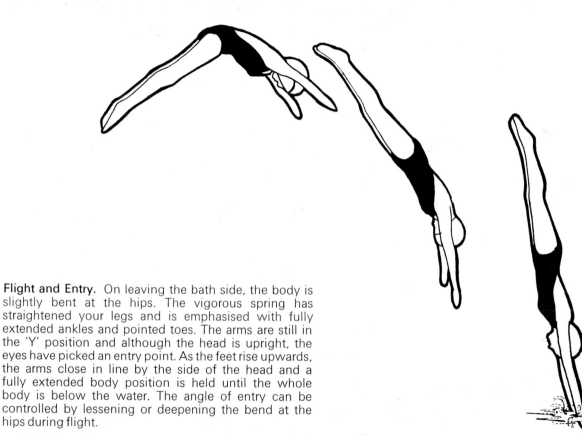

Flight and Entry. On leaving the bath side, the body is slightly bent at the hips. The vigorous spring has straightened your legs and is emphasised with fully extended ankles and pointed toes. The arms are still in the 'Y' position and although the head is upright, the eyes have picked an entry point. As the feet rise upwards, the arms close in line by the side of the head and a fully extended body position is held until the whole body is below the water. The angle of entry can be controlled by lessening or deepening the bend at the hips during flight.

Diving Equipment

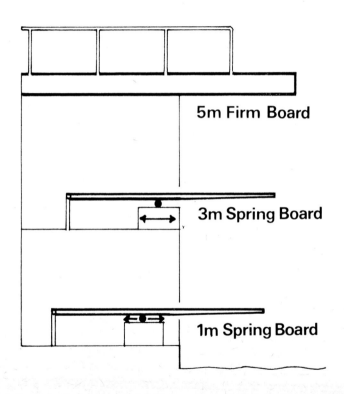

5m Firm Board

3m Spring Board

1m Spring Board

No doubt firmboard diving developed from early leaps from cliffs and rock faces. Today's competitions for firmboards are from five or ten metre boards. The five metre is found in most modern pools and needs a water depth of 3·8 metres, whilst the ten metre is usually found in International Pools with much deeper water.

The modern flexible springboard is used at two heights, one metre and three metres. The official depth of water required for the one metre board is 3 metres, and for the three metres springboard the required depth is 3·5 metres. The best boards are made of aluminimum alloy or wood and glass fibre, and are mounted with a back support and a movable fulcrum. This fulcrum allows the user to adjust the flexibility of the board to suit his requirements.

Standing Springboard Take-off and Straight Jump

Although more height can be attained from a running take-off the standing take-off should be used to learn how arm and leg movements combine to produce maximum thrust into the springboard and greatest lift from the board.

Take up an upright position on the end of the board. Raise the arms upwards and sideways, but avoid a snatched movement. At the same time flex your legs so that you are balanced on the balls of your feet. This will cause the springboard to move upwards. At the top of its rise your arms should move down sideways and behind the hips. Still keeping your weight balanced on the balls of the feet, bend into a crouch. This will coincide with the board being at its lowest point. It is now that the arms should be lifted forcibly to the 'Y' position whilst the legs thrust downwards into the board. This thrust is accompanied with a hard 'ankle snap'. Provided your balance is maintained, the board recoil will propel you upwards. Hold the stretched body position. Keep looking at the far end of the pool and do not lower your head to look at the water. Keep a raised chest, flattened stomach, and keep the toes pointed. Just before the feet enter the water, the arms are lowered to the sides. The entry should be about two feet from the end of the board. The more vigorous your thrust into the board, the more efficiently the board will propel you into the air. Do not look down at the water as a lowered head will put you off balance.

Running Springboard Take-off, Straight Jump

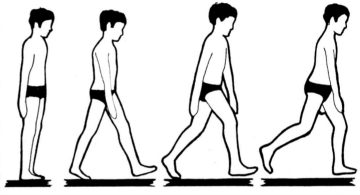

The 'run' of a springboard take-off is in fact a smooth heel and toe walk which must have a minimum of three steps.

It is errors of this take-off which cause most below standard dives. It is imperative therefore that the approach and take off should be constantly practised. The starting position on the board is with a good upright stance, arms to the side, and eyes fixed on the end of the board. The steps along the board should be even and normal and the arm-swing should be kept to a minimum. The last step before alighting on the end of the board is an upward leap. This is caused by one foot pushing hard into the board, whilst both arms are raised to shoulder level or above. Whilst the one foot is pushing and the arms are being lifted, the other leg is raised from the knee, although the toes of that foot are pointed downwards towards the board. The intention is to land on the end of the board in an upright position, on the balls of the feet. The initial push of the board will have caused the board to swing and the leap onto its end will help to increase its downward journey. As feet are about to make contact with the end of the board, your arms should drop downwards and behind your thighs. They should reach this point as your stretched legs bend and you adopt a crouching position. From this point the movements are exactly the same as that for the *standing take-off* and *straight jump*. Remember that you are striving for a landing and

take-off without forward lean. The board will lift you upwards and forward if you let it. Try for height and stretch. The leap onto the board end is called a Hurdle Step. Get a good one and you are half-way to becoming a diver! Practise this approach, hurdle, and jump until your timing is correct. When you are aware that you are getting good lift from the board and that your entries into the water are reasonably clean and stretched, then you should be capable of progressing as a diver.

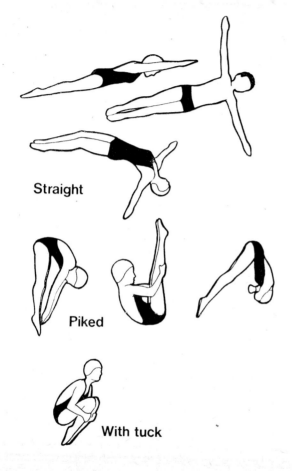

Straight

Piked

With tuck

Diving Positions and Groups

During the flight of the body through the air, the body can be in one of three positions.

Position A. Straight The whole body must be straight, without any bend of hips or knees.

Position B. Piked The body must be bent sharply from the hips, but the legs must be straight.

Position C. Tucked The whole body is bunched into a ball shape, as compactly as possible, with knees bent and together, the hands grasping the legs between knees and ankles.

The Grouping of Dives is as follows :—

1. Forward Group Forward rotation from a forward take-off.

2. Back Group Backward rotation from a back take-off.

3. Reverse Group Backward rotation from a forward take-off.

4. Inward Group Forward rotation from back take-off.

5. Twist Group Any dive in which there is rotation about the long axis of the body.

6. Armstand Group Any dive from the firmboard with an armstand starting position.

Forward Dive, Tucked

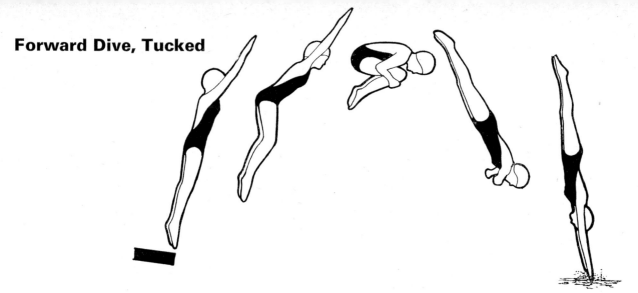

This is the simplest dive of the forward group. It should be learned first of all as it is in fact half of a forward somersault. You can do it either standing or running, whichever you prefer. The take-off is like the already described forward jump take-off, but this time a slight forward lean on take-off initiates a rotating movement. On leaving the board, the legs which have stretched downwards are lifted up, whilst the arms which have stretched upwards are brought down in front and the hands grasp both shins. You are now in a 'tuck' position. This tuck is held until enough rotation is achieved to enable you to spot your entry point. Then open your body out, stretching arms and legs into a straight line which should be held until you reach the bottom of the pool. With a little practise you can eliminate the lean and make an almost vertical lift. The tuck should be done by a sharp inward pull of the hips before the arms and legs 'ball up'. An important point to remember is to keep the head up. Another is to come out of the tuck into a straight position and not an arched one. This dive is an extremely pleasing dive to perform and to watch, provided it is done smoothly.

Forward Dive, Piked

This important dive incorporates the pike position which is part of many advanced dives. It is necessary that the take-off is balanced and without lean. The head should not be lowered as the arms reach above the head. Keep the 'downward press' feeling in your legs, and concentrate on getting a hip lift by a strong pulling upward of the stomach. At this moment the arms should reach downwards to touch the feet which should have the toes pointed as much as possible. The pike position should be clearly shown at the peak of the flight and held until the body has rotated until the entry point is in view. Then the legs are pressed back whilst the arms move towards the entry. Control the stomach muscles when stretching into a straight line so that you avoid swinging into an arched position. Avoid piking too soon, by reaching for the feet as soon as you leave the board. Emphasise the upward arm stretch and the sharp hip lift and, especially on take-off, keep the head up.

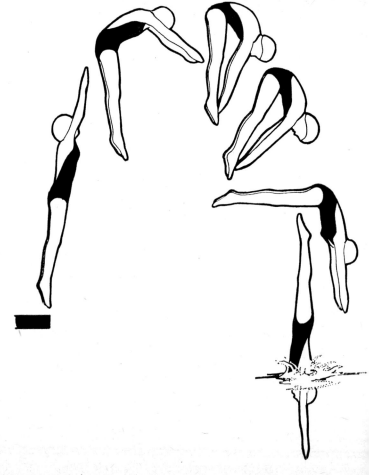

Forward Dive, Straight

This graceful dive, commonly known as the *swallow dive,* looks simple, but it is difficult to perform well as it requires a good take-off and a considerable degree of control. The take-off should be bold, as it is necessary to have a fully straightened body as soon as it leaves the board. The head should be kept in line and the eyes looking to the other end of the pool. Avoid too much lean, and aim for maximum height, reaching upwards with the arms. Then push them sideways so that you are in a 'T' position, with the body fully straightened and the head raised. Do not look down at the water as this will encourage you to bend at the hips, and slow the rise of the feet behind you. You must develop confidence in yourself so that you can hold on to the 'T' position until your stretched body has rotated enough for you to find yourself almost upside down. Then move your arms to line up alongside the head and stretch for the bottom of the pool. Your early dives will probably be with too much lean which may cause you to rotate too much, or, if you have very little height you will not have enough time for rotation and end up with a sort of racing dive. Remember, keep your head up and concentrate on getting your fully stretched legs up behind you.

Backward Springboard Take-off, Straight Jump

This take-off finishes with a body position in the air identical to that for the take-off, straight jump. First of all take up an erect standing position on the end of the board, with the back to the water. The body is supported on the balls of the feet, whilst the heels are clear off the board. Keep your shoulders vertically over your feet, although you may feel that you are leaning forwards too much. Keep well balanced and retain this balance as you raise your arms sideways and upwards. Do not snatch this movement or it will cause your feet to lift off the board which is now moving with you. The purpose of these movements is to get the board moving and to get yourself into a position where you can implant maximum 'push' into the board. Bring your arms down sideways but behind your hips as you bend the knees into a slight crouch position, still with weight over balls of feet. Do not look down. Working in rhythm with the board movements, you will still feel well balanced. When the board has depressed as much as seems possible, you must make a quick effort to depress it further. This is done by moving the arms forwards and upwards at energetic pace. At the same time the legs push downwards as hard as possible with a solid and determined 'ankle snap'! This will cause the board to

lift you upwards and slightly away provided that you have not started to lean back. From then onwards keep the stretch and make a feet first entry in the same way as you have practised for the forward take-off. Remember keep your head up and in line if you want to stay balanced.

Back Dive, Work-ups

As a back dive starts with a position where you cannot see the water, you may feel nervous about going over backwards. If so, you can gain confidence in your own ability by learning the movements in the water. Take up position in the pool as though you are going to start a back stroke race. Push off from the side but instead of swimming, stretch your arms back over your head as though you were going to glide on your back. Then push the arms downwards towards the pool bottom and press your head in the same direction. Make a good arch with your back and endeavour to do a hand-stand on the bottom. After a little practice do it in deeper water and endeavour to do a complete backwards somersault under the water. It is quite easy if you really go for it. You now have that 'going over backwards' feeling. If you still want to take it gradually, the next step is the backwards crouch roll from the bath side. Crouch with back to the water and toes on the edge of the pool, hands grasping the ankles, and head kept forwards. Then roll into the water. Make sure you have adequate depth or you may hit the bottom of the pool with your back. With increasing confidence, go for the crouch roll with an important difference. This time, as you roll and your head approaches the water, straighten the legs, press the head back into the back arch position and reach for the bottom of the pool. Boldness is a necessity, for timidity gives slowness which means that you do not have the time to do the movements. You are now half way to a complete back crouch dive. From the crouch position, start to overbalance but immediately straighten the legs and apply 'ankle snap' to give you lift. At the same time arch the back, throw the arms up and towards the water and look for your entry point. Remember to get that spring into the leg movement so that you get up and away. Push off from the side. Do not just lift the legs off it.

Back Dive, Straight

Before attempting the complete dive, the *back crouch dive* should be repeated on the one metre springboard, with the fulcrum rolled well forward to avoid getting too much spring. To adjust for the additional height, you must endeavour to get a controlled 'turn-over' movement, so do not topple too far backwards before pushing. Look for your entry point and push through it.

To do a proper back dive you must now go back to the backwards take-off with the plain jump. The take-off for the dive is identical until the push off from the board. Now the emphasis is on getting the chest up high to achieve the arched back and this is the objective as the arms swing forwards and upwards. The legs are pressed downwards as though you are attempting to push the board into the water. The head is lifted back so that you can see the water. As you lift off the board, the arms spread into a 'T' position. When you see your entry point (and it is quite quickly) close your arms into an extended position slightly behind your head, and keep a fully stretched body until you are under the water. Do not obey a natural instinct to lean back towards the water or you may turn over too much if you have any height from the board, or go half way along the pool if you have no lift. Remember, the object is to push the board downwards so that the board will propel you upwards ! Keep a high chest and a good stretch and look where you are going.

Back Dive, Piked

Some people find it easier to perform a back dive in this position for the body turns quicker when in the pike position than when straight. However, you must first experiment on the bath side to see which you prefer. If you have poor flexibility in the hips, keep to the straight position. If you have no difficulty in touching your toes whilst keeping the legs straight, then take up this position on the pool side with your back to the water. Now grasp the ankles, and without bending your legs, topple back into the water seat first. Keep your head forwards. If you are confident that you can easily adopt this position, you can progress to the pool side back pike jump. Stand erect on the pool edge, back to the water and jump upwards and slightly away. It is important that the arms are lifted upwards as you take off. Now pull the hips back and grasp your ankles so that you are in the pike position and once more do a seat first entry. Remember, you are trying to land on your seat, not on your back! When you are sure of your pike movement, you can get on the springboard for the dive. The take-off is similar to the pike jump backwards but with a very slight lean. Swing the arms upwards as your feet drive into the board. Keep the head in line, and do not lower it or lift it. Feel the arms stretching in line with your ears and concentrate on moving the hips back so that your fully stretched legs will lift into the pike position. When the body, still in the pike position, has rotated so that your feet are pointing upwards, move into a straight position (which

will slow down your turning movement) and look for, and stretch your arms and body through your water entry point. On taking off for this dive concentrate on good balance on the board so that you are in a position to really push to obtain time in the air. Complete the movements with a nicely lined up entry.

Inward Dive, Tucked

This dive is a combination of the backward take-off and the *forward dive, tucked.* Your immediate problem is to overcome the natural nervousness you may feel about doing a dive where you have to go towards the board. You must realise that if you have a bold thrusting movement into the springboard and you are in balance, the board will lift you up and away. Do some back jump take-offs and concentrate on entering the water a few feet back from the board. Do not, however, snatch your feet away on take-off as this will bring your upper body forwards towards the board. You are aiming for a very slight angle to the vertical. Repeat this movement until you can confidently enter the water at almost 45 degrees, a few feet away from the board. When this skill has been obtained, you are ready for the next step. All you have to do is repeat your movement, but this time increase the hip lift by pulling your stomach inwards. Lower your head, grasp the ankles, and pull your body into a nicely tucked position. Hold this position and enter the water in a 'bomb'. You can now complete the final step. This time go for the tucked position but make it high enough to give you time to rotate. When you see your entry point, straighten the body out and stretch for the bottom. Remember to reach the arms up on take-off, for whilst they are going upwards, your feet are pushing downwards and the result is a nice high line of flight with time for a good entry. Keep the head up, so that you can see where you are going.

Inward Dive, Piked

The technique for this dive is similar to the *inward dive tucked,* but as the body rotates slightly slower in the piked position, more emphasis must be made on the 'hip lifting' movement. The take-off is as the *inward tuck dive* but the legs are firmly pressed downwards when the arms move into the 'Y' position, and every effort is made to lift the hips up and to the rear when the arms move downwards to touch the toes. This pike position should be reached when you are at the peak of the dive. Keep the toes pointed downwards and try to prevent your feet from flying back. Feel as though your feet are staying in the same spot whilst your hips are rising. Keep your head up so that you do not rush into the pike before you have enough height from board. Hold the tight pike position until you have rotated enough to spot your entry point. Straighten the body by a controlled stretch which should start from the stomach. Squeeze the legs together as they lift, and move the top half of the body forwards as the arms line up by the side of your head. If your timing is correct you should end up with a nicely stretched entry. Remember, keep the head up on take-off, thrust hard into the board and reach upwards and in front of your head. Concentrate on lifting your hips, do not snatch your legs backwards.

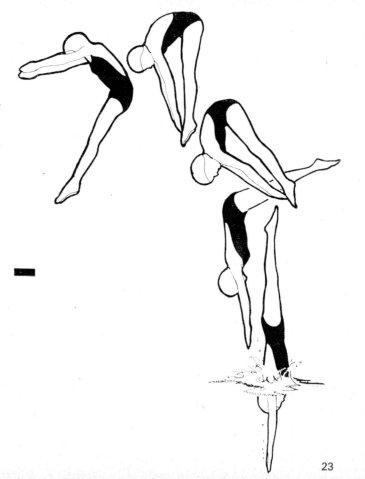

Reverse Jump

The reverse dive has backward rotation from a forward take-off. This is not a natural movement for most people and preparatory work-ups help to get the feel of the movement and establish confidence in your own ability. It is first necessary to learn how to safely clear the board and yet be turning towards it. Start on the pool side. Put one foot on the bath side, toes gripping the edge. Move the other leg back as though you are preparing to kick a ball. Place the arms in line behind your hips. Swing the arms forward vigorously with the rear leg moving forwards in a kicking motion. Keep the head up. Concentrate your gaze on your own hands which will have moved up above the head with fully extended arms. Your swinging arms have implanted a turning motion to your body. The intention is to get the feel of this turning motion, not to get you landing on your back. Your line of flight should be up and safely away from the bath side, Keep the arms in the 'Y' position and aim to enter the water feet first but laying back at an angle of about 45 degrees. When you have mastered this and are confident, you can take the next step towards the complete dive.

Reverse Dive, Walk-off

Use either the one metre springboard or a firmboard. If you use a springboard do not have the fulcrum too far back as it will need more control. Remember that you are now farther away from the water and therefore have more time to turn. Stand one step back from the end and swing into the reverse movement you have already mastered. The difference is that this time you are going to go further round into a head first entry. The rear foot is kicked forwards more vigorously and the arm swing is also applied with more power. The head is pulled back to look for the water and the arms move from the 'Y' position to the shoulder level 'T' position. The moving of the arms has shortened the body length which in turn speeds up the turning action which the arm swing has started. The body should be stretched with emphasis on chest lift. When the legs move upwards and the head is down towards the water, the arms should close in line for entry. It is essential that the take-off has no lean back towards the board, or that the head is not pressed back until the forward kick movement is completed. With increasing confidence, the aim should be to increase your time in the air by getting more height, and to increase control of the flight of the dive. The arching of the back should be accomplished by a lifted chest, not by throwing the hips forwards, for this encourages dragging legs and lack of height. What you are attempting to do is not easy, so get the early stages right.

Reverse Dive, Straight

Start with a running take-off, alighting on the end of the board in an upright position. Your arm swing should be deeper and more vigorous for you are going to instil plenty of turn. Your leg thrust is extended downwards and this downwards pressure is maintained throughout the dive. Do not lower your head and keep a high chest. Accentuate the arm swing and you will feel the hips and legs moving forwards and upwards. As the body moves up to the peak of the flight the head should be dropped back so that you see the board and your entry point in the water. At the same time the arms should move to the 'T' position, which is held until the arms close in line for your entry. Your body should have an arched, but stretched position. In your early attempts for safety you will obviously take the dive well forward from the board, no doubt by leaning on take-off. The usual follow up of this is a lunge forward of the hips, which will ensure an arched turning body but not enough time for a good entry line. Avoid the natural tendency to rush into a swinging arch. Try to imagine yourself in the air in a horizontal position with plenty of height, about three feet from the end of the board. Then make every effort to place yourself in this position. Stay upright when you land on the end of the board. Get a good, solid arm swing, push the board hard. Do not lean back on take-off and do not throw your head back before you are away from the board. These are the two things which bring your dive too near the board. This is an easy and safe dive provided you make sure of your take-off and are confident of your movements.

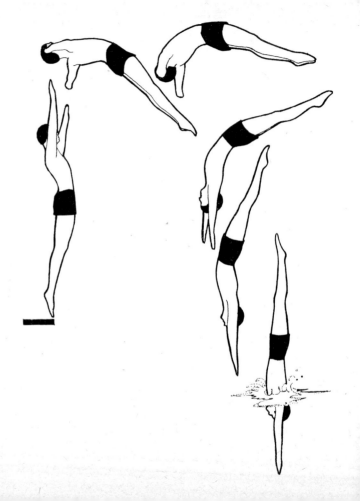

Reverse Dive, Piked

Once you are in the air this dive has the same movements as the *back dive, piked,* so if you prefer a back dive in this position you will have no problems with your reverse pike. From the take-off the arms swing powerfully upwards in a very definite swing. Try to visualise it stopping as your arms are extended on each side of your forehead. This swing and reach will help you to stretch your toes hard into the board, which you should leave almost as though you were attempting to do a reverse jump straight, but with very little turn of the body. The head should remain still and you should endeavour to look at your hands. Make sure that your hips do not move forwards, for they should now be pulled in as the stretched legs lift upwards and your hands press to the feet. This sharp piking will speed up the slow turn which was present in your initial take-off and you will find yourself in the same position you are in half way through your back dive piked. The only difference is that this time you will see the board from the piked to the entry position. Make sure that you lift your chest when you move into line and keep the stomach pulled in. The reverse dive turning motion is faster piked than straight. You must learn just how long to hold on to the pike so that your body extension is right for your entry line.

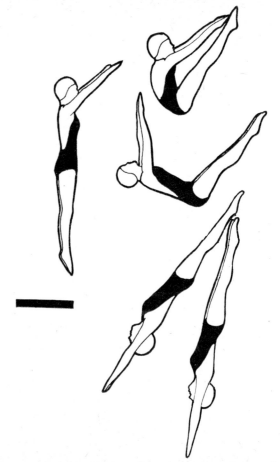

Forward Dive, Half Twist

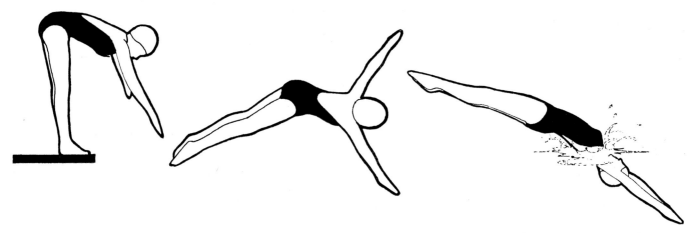

An easy description of this dive is a *forward dive straight* with a twist about the long axis of the body. This is a simple picture of a dive which is far from easy for the beginner to perform efficiently, as it requires control of forward rotation and twist. You must work on your *forward dive straight* until you can perform it with reasonable proficiency before you attempt to add the twist. It will also help if you get the feel of the movement before going for the complete dive. To do this you should stand on the end of a low board as though you were doing a pike fall. Stretch the arms out as you do in the 'T' position. Then, keeping the arms extended, move one shoulder so that one arm is pointing towards the entry point directly in front of the board. Move the other arm a little, so that it is near your side and to the rear. Look at the entry point and topple forward, extending the forward arm for the entry. As you topple, the other arm is lifted behind your head which is kept raised. The rear shoulder should press back and you will find yourself in a back dive straight position. You should still be looking at the entry point. You may turn in either direction, so lead with whichever arm suits you. Practise this 'falling cartwheel' action until it can be performed smoothly. The take-off for the complete dive is like that for the *forward dive straight*, but instead of placing the body in a parallel position in mid-air, you should attempt to place it in the same place, but with a slight angle on it. It should NOT go to the side of the board. If you aim for this, you will have put the twisting action in your body as you leave the board. Do not try for a vicious twisting movement. Look out along the pool as you set up your slightly angled 'T' position.

Without lowering the head, glance along the arm which is moving down towards the water. The other arm keeps fully extended as it rises. Now, without lowering your head, look for your entry point. Your body must maintain a fully stretched, slightly arched position. By this time your twisting motion will have turned you almost into a back dive straight position, and if you are still looking at your entry point, your head will now be lifted. It is now that your arms close in line with the side of the head as in the *back dive straight*. In your early efforts at the *forward dive half twist*, try to avoid a too obvious twisting motion from the board. Only a slight amount of twisting action is needed and you will learn to slow it by keeping the arms spread, or quicken it by closing the arms. Make certain that you do not lower your head or this will encourage a tendency to 'pike', which will of course really spoil your entry line.

Keep the legs fully stretched until you are right under the water, and avoid leaning forward when you take-off.

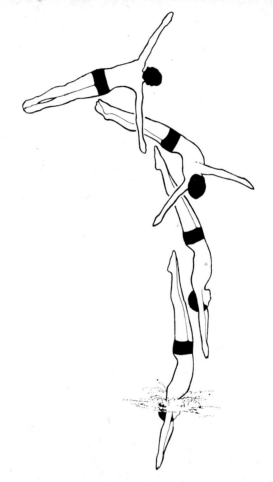

Learning the Forward Somersault

Performing a somersault is the first ambition of most aspiring divers, and the forward somersault is the easiest to master. You have realised that in the *forward dive tucked* you have in fact done half a somersault, so you go back to this simple tuck position as a starting point. Crouch on the pool side in a tuck position, toes gripping the edge. Keep tightly balled up with knees close together, and roll forward into the water. Keep a tight grasp of the shins and hold tight until you are right under the water. You must practise this until you are confident you can roll right over without letting go of your legs. Now you can take the next step which is again from the pool side. This time, stand on the edge in a slightly crouched position, with arms forward but bent, so that the hands are almost at face level. Your

object is to once more 'roll over' but this time above and not in the water. Start a slight lean forward, then throw the arms hard downwards, drop the chin onto the chest and drive the hips upwards. This hip drive can only be achieved by a hard thrusting action of the legs and plenty of 'ankle thrust'. Your hands must grasp the ankles and you must avoid the tendency to come out of the tucked position too soon, or you will land on your back. If you are worried that this might occur, you should wear a sweater. However, if you make up your mind that you are going to go for the somersault with a real one hundred per cent effort, and use your legs to get your hips up, you will find that a somersault from the pool side is easy, and that a seat and feet landing is no problem.

The Forward Somersault

Once you can achieve a feet first entry from a pool side somersault you need have no worries about performing from a one metre springboard. You have more time to complete your somersault as you have additional distance from the water before you start your dive, plus the extra height which the board recoil will give you. Your approach and take-off are the same as that for the *forward tuck dive*, only this time you are going to get that extra bit of turn which you have just learned to obtain. For your early attempts, do not try for too much turning movement. Hold on to a tight tuck, even if you go into the water 'balled up'. Aim for feeling the hips going up and over. Keep the eyes open and attempt to come out of the tuck into the straight position when you are looking at the far end of the pool.

You can get a friend to give you a shout at the moment when you should stretch out for the entry. Keep the head still, and your arms must be by your sides and not above your head. Make up your mind that you are not going to lean too far forward on take-off. Remember you want time to turn and to stretch, so get up as high as you can. Extra lean gives extra turn and you want your turn to be under control. You will soon be aware of your position during somersaults, whether you are upside down or right way up, so practise. Remember, one good turn deserves another.

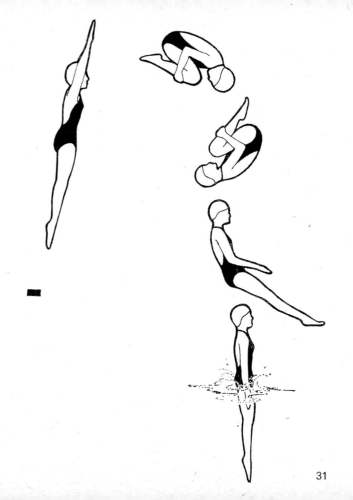

Forward Dive with One Twist

The greatest number of dives in any group of dives, are those in the Twist group. In the *forward dive with half twist* you learned how taking off and attempting to set the body at a slight angle caused you to apply twisting action to the body. This twisting action was created before your feet left the board and, in fact, if you had been diving from a very high board it would have been impossible to stop your twisting movement. Now we are going to move on to a twisting dive where you do not start twisting until you are well clear of the board. The technique of creating twist in mid-air is used in the *forward dive with one twist*.

You can learn the basic requirements by once more returning to the pool side. First of all you must practise jumping into a 'Y' position, but with a slight pike at the hips. At the peak of your jump the twist is brought about by pulling back one shoulder so that one arm is positioned behind the head. The other arm, bent at the elbow, is pulled across to front of chest. Whilst these arm actions are being performed, the legs are pressed down to a firmly stretched position. This will remove the slight pike which your body had on take off, and the firm lower half of your body will act as the pivot for the twisting motion which your arms and shoulders had instigated. Your head should follow round with the shoulder which has pulled to the rear and you will find yourself looking in the direction of the elbow of that arm. Like the *half-twist*, whether you turn clockwise

or anti-clockwise is entirely a matter of personal preference so make up your mind which way you prefer before you move on to the complete dive. Remember that when you are doing this jump, the twisting action is done at the peak. Get a friend to call 'twist' when you are clear of the pool side, but he should not call on every take-off—then you will discover whether or not you are really waiting until you are in mid-air. When you are sure that you can twist without taking any twist call from the pool side, then you can move to the spring-board for the *forward dive with one twist*. The take-off for this dive is like the *plain header*, which was one of your earliest dives. The initial flight position from the

the board must have the arms in the 'Y' position, with the shoulders relaxed inwards. This will give you a slightly rounded upper spine. You must also have the slight 'pike' at the hips. These factors are extremely important for it is the slightly relaxed upper half of the body which is going to twist against the rigid lower half of the body. As you leave the board with minimum forward lean, your arms snap into the twisting action you have already mastered in your pool side jumps. Your lower half of the body is pressed into line to assist the pirouette of the twist. The arms are held in the twisting position until a complete twist has almost been achieved. When you see water your arms should stretch momentarily to the 'Y' position, then they will press into line for a clean entry. This dive takes a lot of practice to obtain the smooth precision which makes it attractive, so rehearse the arm movements and the pirouette as often as you can. You do not need water or a springboard for this. Keep the head movements to the minimum and you will avoid that 'getting lost' feeling during twisting. Avoid too much lean on take off and set the initial *plain header* slightly short in turn. In other words, take-off as though your final entry line is going to be less steep than usual—the slightly piked position during flight will turn you faster for a short period and will steepen your angle for entry after the twist.

Armstand Dive

One group of dives can be performed only from a firmboard. This is the group where the starting position is from an armstand. The armstand should be well practised on firm ground, preferably against a wall, or with the help of a friend. The arms must be kept straight and the fingers should press down hard when you are balancing so that you can move your body back into line if you start overbalancing. Try not to get an arched back, and keep the legs squeezed together with the toes curled back. When you can stand on your hands, you can attempt an entry into the water from this position, but make it from the low board.

Lift up to a balance, with the hands on the edge, finger tips pressing hard. Let the body overbalance slightly, keeping the arms straight. Push off and away from the side with the hands to bring the shoulders vertically beneath the feet to make an upright entry.

When you are confident on the low board, the dive can be taken from the higher boards, with deeper water. The movements are the same but do not overbalance too far or push too vigorously with the hands or you will lose control.

Do not lift the head, but use your eyes to spot the entry point.

Armstand with Forward Cut Through

This dive should be learned in the tuck position. It is assumed that you are now capable of holding your balance for a second or two. Once again, from an armstand, the overbalancing action is begun. Make sure that your shoulders are kept well forward, and as your feet move from their point of balance, your eyes should look at your entry point in the water. However, at the very moment of losing balance, the shoulders are pushed forward, the eyes maintaining their gaze at the water. At the same moment your body pulls into the tuck position. The push forward of the shoulders as your legs move down into the tuck position will cause your body to rotate so that your shoulders and head move up towards the ceiling over the pool, whilst the lower part of your tucked body rotates downwards. There will not be a tremendous amount of turn created and it is necessary to hold this tucked position until quite near the water. The object is to time the stretch out of the tuck so that you obtain a nicely lined up entry position, with arms by the sides and fully extended legs. Don't lower your head as you move out of the tucked position but make sure your eyes are spotting your entry point.

Competitive Diving

Diving in competition is the object of serious training. It is the only sure way of measuring your progress and the standard of your diving. Contests at School and Club level will usually involve simple dives like the *plain header*, but at County, District and higher levels, the competitions will require dives to be selected from some or all of the diving groups. The judges of these contests will be looking to see if the technical requirements of the dives are met, for efficient use of the springboard, correct body position and line of flight and a clean, near vertical entry. Added to these requirements of a dive are two qualities which make the difference between an average dive and one which is aesthetically pleasing to an onlooker—grace and beauty. Judges of diving contests award marks from 0 to 10 in half marks. All dives have an officially graded 'degree of difficulty' ranging from $1 \cdot 1$ to $3 \cdot 0$.

High marks can be earned for difficult dives provided, of course, that they are performed well. To quote an example, a diver is performing an *inward one and a half somersault* from the three metre springboard, in the tucked position. The 'Degree of Difficulty' for this dive is $2 \cdot 0$. We have five judges whose marks awarded are $4\frac{1}{2}$, 5, 5, $5\frac{1}{2}$, 6. To obtain a fair average, both the highest and the lowest scores are removed and the remaining three scores are added together—in this case 5, 5, $5\frac{1}{2}$—giving a total of $15\frac{1}{2}$. This is now multiplied by the difficulty value and we have a final score for the dive of 31.00. In selecting dives for a contest the competitor may prefer to use an easier dive which he can perform to a high standard, rather than risk using a more difficult one which he might perform inadequately.

Conduct of Competitions—Judging

All recognised diving competitions under the laws of the Amateur Swimming Association are governed by F.I.N.A. Regulations. Some of the more important laws concerning the execution and judging of dives are given as follows :—

Rule 98. Points or half points shall be awarded from 0–10 according to the opinion of the judges and the following table :

Completely failed	0 point
Unsatisfactory	$\frac{1}{2}$–2 points
Deficient	$2\frac{1}{2}$–$4\frac{1}{2}$,,
Satisfactory	5 –6 ,,
Good	$6\frac{1}{2}$–8 ,,
Very Good	$8\frac{1}{2}$–10 ,,

Rule 99. When judging a dive only the dive is to be considered without regard to the approach to the starting position. The points to be considered are :

The run

The take-off

The technique and grace of the dive during the passage through the air.

The entry into the water.

Execution of the Dive

Rule 104. Dives should be executed and judged on the following principles:

(a) The approach to the starting position shall not be taken into consideration; the starting position shall be free and unaffected.

(b) The starting position in standing dives shall be assumed when the competitor stands on the front end of the board or on the front end of the platform. The body shall be straight, head erect, with the arms straight and to the sides or above the head. The arm swing commences when the arms leave the starting position.

If the correct starting position is not assumed, each judge shall deduct 1 to 3 points from his award, according to circumstances. The starting position of a running dive shall be assumed when the competitor is ready to take the first step of the run.

Forward take-off dives from the springboard may be performed either standing or running at the option of the diver. A prior declaration of the manner of take-off is not required. The judges shall award points for a standing dive bearing in mind the height and standard of execution which might be expected from a running dive. After the competition is started a diver may not bounce on the springboard until after the score of the previous diver has been announced.

(c) The run shall be smooth, straight and without hesitation. In a running dive from either the springboard or the platform the diver shall take at least four steps in all, including the take-off from one or both feet.

If the diver takes less than four steps the referee shall deduct two points from the award of each judge.

(d) The take-off shall be bold, reasonably high and confident. In running dives the take-off from the springboard must be from both feet simultaneously or the referee shall declare it a failed dive, but from fixed boards the take-off can be from one foot only. When executing a standing dive, the diver must not bounce on the board before the take-off.

When executing a running dive, the diver shall not be allowed to stop his run before the end of the board and to make more than one jump on the same spot, before the final take-off, or the referee shall declare it a failed dive. If a diver, preparing for the take-off in backward dives, lifts his feet slightly off the board, this shall not be regarded as a bounce, but as an involuntary movement and the judges (not the referee) shall deduct from their awards according to their individual opinions.

If in any dive the diver touches the end of the board, or dives to the side of the direct line of flight this indicates, no matter how well the dive may have been executed, that he was too close to the board for proper execution and each judge must exercise his own opinion regarding the deduction to be made.

If, in an Armstand Dive, a steady balance in the straight position is not shown the judges should deduct from 1 to 3 points.

The diver who loses his balance and who makes a second attempt shall receive 2 points less than if he had obtained his balance at the first attempt. This deduction shall not be made by the judges but shall be announced by the referee, who shall subtract 2 points from the award of each judge or from the average value of their awards. If the second attempt to obtain a balance is unsuccessful, the referee shall declare it as a failed dive.

The same applies to a re-start in a standing dive after the arm swing has commenced or to a re-start in a running after the run has commenced.

On the occasion of strong wind, the referee may give all competitors the right to make a re-start without deduction of points. This should, if possible be announced before the Commencement of the contest.

(e) During the passage through the air the body can be carried straight, with pike or with tuck. In the first case the body shall not be bent either at the knees, or at the hips, the feet shall be together and the toes pointed.

In the second case the body shall be bent at the hips, but the legs must be kept straight at the knees, toes pointed. In the third case the whole body is bunched up with the knees together, hands on the lower legs and toes pointed.

If a diver opens his knees in the tuck, the judges shall deduct from one to two points.

The diving illustrations serve as guides only and it is to be noted that the position of the arms shall be at the choice of the diver. The position of the arms in the Forward Dive Straight shall now be optional as for all the other movements. The beauty of the dive shall be a matter for the judges.

(f) In all flying somersaults dives a straight position should be clearly shown for approximately half a somersault.

(g) In straight dives with one half or full twist, the twisting must not manifestly be done from the board.

In pike dives with twist, the twist must not be started until there has been a marked pike position. In somersault dives with twist, the twist may be performed at any time during the dive at the option of the competitor.

(h) The entry into the water must in all cases be vertical, or nearly so, with the body straight, toes pointed. All head first entries shall be executed with the arms stretched beyond the head in a line with the body, with the hands close together ; all feet first entries with the arms close to the body, and no bending at the elbows.

If the arms are not in the correct prescribed position on entry into the water, each judge shall deduct from 1 to 3 points from his award according to circumstances.

If the arms are held beyond the head in a feet first entry the dive is not to be considered as satisfactory. The highest award for such a dive shall be $4\frac{1}{2}$ points.

The dive is considered to be finished when the whole body is completely under the surface of the water.

Proficiency Awards for Diving

As your diving improves, you can take various proficiency awards organised by the Amateur Swimming Association. These tests are given below. Full details can be obtained from the A.S.A. Central Office, Harold Fern House, Derby Sq., Loughborough, Leicestershire, LE11 0AL.

Elementary
GRADE I

From the Bathside
1. Plain Header
2. Forward Dive, piked or tucked
3. Back Jump, tucked

GRADE II

From a 4 foot firmboard or 1 metre springboard
1. Plain Header
2. Forward Dive, piked or tucked
3. Inward Dive, piked or tucked
4. Back Dive, piked, tucked or straight
   Dives of the same number shall count as the same dives.

Bronze Standard

Ladies and Men. Five voluntary dives from a one or three metre springboard, selected from at least three different groups. The whole test must be performed from the same board height.

Dives of the same number shall count as the same dive.

Silver Standard, Springboard

Ladies and men: six voluntary dives.

All from a one or three metre springboard and selected from at least five different groups.

The whole test must be performed from the same board height.

Dives of the same number shall count as the same dive.

Silver Standard, High Board

Ladies: Five voluntary dives from a five metre board selected from at least four different groups.

Men: Six voluntary dives from a five metre board, selected from at least five different groups.

Dives of the same number shall count as the same dive.

Gold Standard, Springboard

Ladies: Ten voluntary dives from a three metre springboard, two dives to be selected from each group.

Men: Ten voluntary dives from a three metre springboard, two dives to be selected from each group.

Dives of the same number shall count as the same dive.

Gold Standard, High Board

Ladies: Three voluntary dives from ten metres, and three voluntary dives from five or ten metres, selected from at least four different groups.

Men: Eight voluntary dives from ten metres, five of which must be selected, one from each group.

In judging the tests, degrees of difficulty shall not be taken into consideration. The judge's awards shall be aggregated, and the following percentages shall be required to obtain a pass :—

Bronze, 40 per cent.

Silver, 45 per cent.

Gold, 55 per cent.

Dives of the same number shall count as the same dive.

Printed by The White Rose Press, Mexborough and London